Wearing Johnny's Shirt

And Other Poems

Copyright © 2018 by Ken Vance, all rights reserved. No part of this book may be reproduced, stored or transmitted in any form or by any means without written permission from Ken Vance and/or ThomasMax Publishing. An exception is granted for brief excerpts taken for review purposes.

ISBN-13: 978-0-9994538-5-8
ISBN-10: 0-9994538-5-8

Front and back cover photos courtesy of Joe Grant.

First printing: November 2018

Published by:

ThomasMax Publishing
P O B 250054
Atlanta, GA 30325
thomasmax.com

Wearing Johnny's Shirt
And Other Poems

Ken Vance

ThomasMax

Your Publisher
For The 21st Century

ACKNOWLEDGMENTS

I would like to offer my special thanks to Ms. Susan Lindsley, author and poet, for her help and encouragement that led to the publication of this book.

Dedication

To the late Dr. Betty Sellers,

My wonderful wife, Carol,

And the "Boss," Dr. G!

None of this would have happened

Without these three women.

Foreword

I began writing back in the late 60's in high school. I called it "piddlin,'" something to pass the time or impress the girls. I wasn't serious about it, but the idea of language and the music of words being put together for a reason started to sprout in me. Then, when I was a senior at Rabun Gap-Nacoochee School, I began to read poets like Keats and James Dickey, Milton, Shakespeare, and Allen Ginsburg, and the whole idea of poetry and the economy of words went from that earlier sprout to a deep root. I started keeping a journal, one of those black and white, wide line notebooks you find in stores in the school supply section. I tried to write everyday but between milking cows every morning, school, and basketball I wasn't that prolific. Still, it was my way of getting away with myself and coming to terms with social issues, the Vietnam War and draft dodgers, hormones, and Jesus.

Upon graduation and holding a high draft number, I enrolled in Young Harris College and met Dr. Betty Sellers, a poet herself, who would become the Poet Laurate of Georgia under Governor Zell Miller. She made me write. She made me learn the names of mountain flora and why the mountain peaks and streams had names like Hightower Bald and Bearmeat Creek. She instilled in me the appreciation for the music of words and phrases and the idea of "making it new." I published a few poems in the college literary magazine, The Corn Creek Review, with titles like "Can Kickin' Kids" and "Woodstove Lament."

After YHC, I went to the University of Georgia and became a certified Law Enforcement Officer through a federally funded program there. I also attended classes and worked toward a degree in English. There I began reading novels like the Great Gatsby, The Sun Also Rises, more Shakespeare, and the plays of Arthur Miller and Tennessee Williams. I left UGA and began my law enforcement career with the Monroe Police Department in 1975 as a patrol officer then went to Florida to buy drugs as a contract agent for the feds. After getting shot at enough I went back to Monroe PD. One night I went to work my shift and the dispatcher, Mrs. June, handed me an application to Georgia College in Milledgeville and told me to fill it out and she would pay the fee to apply. She told me that I was going to finish my college degree and that was that. I did as I was told and got accepted for the fall quarter of 1976.

That fall I took off down Hwy. 441 to Milledgeville in a 1954 two-door Chevrolet named "Walt." I still remember seeing the smoke stacks at Plant Harley Branch and wondering what kind of industrial location I was heading to. Turns out that the plant was about the only industry around. Milledgeville was known as the home of "crazy people," and I was going to school there. I checked into to Beeson Dorm and met Pierre, (French for Nate) my room-mate from Moultrie.

It was at Georgia College where my writing got another gear because of an English teacher named Dr. Sarah Gordon. My writing matured I guess you could say. She made understand how important the ear is to poetry, and that it is through the ear that you develop your voice, and I did develop my voice as she pulled me kicking and screaming through Robert Penn Warren, Wendell Berry, Maxine Kumin, Miller Williams, more James Dickey, and the novelist and essayist, Walker Percy, who strangely enough bears a strong resemblance to my grandfather, Johnny Bolton.

That voice, and the voice that you will read in these pages comes from writing about what I know and sometimes imagine as I come to terms with those things that have become me. That voice got me accepted to the Creative Writing Program at the University of Arkansas where I studied under Miller Williams, James Whitehead, Howard Nemerov, and other big timers.

Now I am in my 44th year as a lawman, having worked in Georgia, Florida, and Arkansas as either a state or local officer. Guess I am still that "poet with a gun" that I was once referred to in an Atlanta Constitution newspaper article. I hope you enjoy these musings, and I will continue to piddle in another one of those black and white speckled notebooks.

Home

Is a man's home his birthplace? If not, then where is it? Is his home a physical structure on measurable acreage, or is it a state of mind? Are there people of a certain area whose influence and tenderness make a man feel at home, and finally, with a nod to the cliché, is home where the heart is? I have an idea that all of these questions are true in degrees; nevertheless, there is a need for a personal definition, a personal account of the author's own idea of home, where it is, its cast of players, and whether or not the author has in his own consciousness an idea of that real or imagined place called home.

For me, home is where all the assets and liabilities that are me originated. It is that place in South Georgia where 12 years of my biography are woven into pine needles, lightard stumps, and black porous soil. My home is a collage of particular sounds, people, and memories; but above all, it is that very small physical place with an enormous emotional foundation.

The house was a small, weathered grey white pine structure in the southeast section of Turner County, Georgia on the left-hand side of Denham Rd., about 7 and half miles east of the city limit sign of Sycamore. It stood surrounded on 3 sides by barbed wire fence and creosote posts.

The house had 6 small rooms: a living room with a green vinyl easy chair and couch, one end table with a radio tuned to WSM in Nashville, Tennessee, the station which provided the family's entertainment on Friday and Saturday nights. There was a wood heater with a black stack that reached through the ceiling. In the corner was always a pile of dry kindling wood. Behind the living room was the kitchen that contained a sink with faucets but no running water, a four-foot galvanized metal table with 6 matching chairs, an electric stove, and a cabinet attached to the wall above and to the left of the stove. To the left of the kitchen was "the chifforobe room" where Mama had some of her old clothes and most of her china in large Kleenex boxes. In their midst was an oak dining table covered with a white bed sheet; all hidden and boxed until we could move into something better, and a refrigerator that was on the right just inside the room's entrance. Adjoining "the chifforobe room" was one of the two "half rooms," appropriately named because they were about half the size of the other rooms. In this room was a dresser with an oval mirror, more Kleenex boxes of memorabilia, the slop jar, and a make shift closet where Mama hung her long Eastern Star gowns and other dresses protected by a rainbow- colored Indian blanket that she bought in Oklahoma at the end of her last marriage.

In front of this room was the other "half room" where my brother, Otis, read Tarzan books and slept in a double bed. Because of the size of this room and the size of Otis's bed, there was little space for anything other than the gun rack that Uncle Harold had given him on his tenth birthday.

Lastly, connecting Otis's room to the living room was the bedroom where Mama, my sister Suzi, and I slept. Mama and Suzi had a double bed with a feather mattress, and I had a single bed with an iron frame and squeaky springs. The house had 3 doors: a front and back door and a door between the living room and the big bedroom. There was a front and back porch, windows in every room, linoleum floors. My house was this, but my home was more.

Apart from the physical structure of my house was 'the place' as farmers called it, or the lot where the house set. The place proper had two mimosa trees in front of the house and a peach tree behind the house with a combination smoke house, chicken coop, and a canned vegetable pantry beside the tree. Deep in the back yard and next to the fence was an outhouse where my brother kept his girlie magazines and his collection of *Outdoor Life* magazines. That was the place proper, but there was more.

Across the road was Collie's pond where Otis and I used to swim naked at dusk in late May before the city pool opened. There was a pine thicket in the back pasture where I made forts and sang love songs to the girls I had recently discovered. There was the "branch" next to Randy Myers' where he and I caught red-eye perch with our bare hands. And of course, there were the fields, planted, fallow, and pastured where the farmers' livelihood depended on each harrowed clod of dirt and a good stand of grazing oats for Angus and Hereford cattle. There is more....

There were the people... people reared in the agrarian ideal and the Bible Belt. There was LaRue and Aubrey Lee Myers and their two sons, Ronnie and Randy, who owned a farm of 400 or so acres. LaRue cared for the livestock and empty, dinner-time stomachs; Aubrey Lee ran the farm machinery, and they took turns worrying in the off years when the crops or prices or both were particularly bad.

There were Collie and Effie Cleghorn; Collie wasn't much of a farmer but he had a hellacious wildlife collection. He had a good assortment of deer, bobcats, 'possums, and racoons and two novelty animals: a bear that drank RC colas, and a baboon that openly played with his privates. Mrs. Cleghorn sewed quilts and shawls and called Collie an "old fool."

There were Granny and Grand-daddy who also had a medium sized farm which they rented out to other farmers seeking acreage, but Granddaddy plowed a five-acre tract for a garden between his house and ours with a grey mule named Buster that never obeyed him. Through his verbal bouts with Buster at the end of each row I learned to cuss at an early age.

The quality that all these folks had in common was an unwavering trust in God which cast a spell on me that I am under to this day. To be sure, their lives were affected by progress (they had a television) but the effect was gradual. They seemed to hold Time with tight reigns; they guided it, it guided them, and both sides benefited from the exchange. These were men who wore overalls and khakis everyday except Sunday and at funerals, and women who wore dungarees that zipped on the left side and who shaved their legs only on Saturday night or Sunday morning, and children who were reared under the rigors of daily chores and peach tree switches. They were all part of my home, but my home was more.

There were the sounds of home…Sparrows and bats nesting in the attic…Bees making honey in the front wall of Otis's bedroom…The occasional rat gnawing the cardboard and cellophane from around the saltine crackers in the cabinet... The noisy kingfisher sitting atop the power line excited by his recent catch...Diesel tractors toiling in late August to pull combines and corn pickers from row to row... The angus bull bellowing in heat or pawing the ground and snorting an answer to another bull's challenge... A boar hog rubbing his hams against a worn fence post in the feed lot...A 'coon dog treeing his prey near midnight... Collie's baboon crying from homesickness... The sound of flushed quail wings straining for flight... The largemouth bass breaking water and catching a dragonfly by surprise... The sound of Grand-daddy's double barrel as he chastised a hog for rooting out of the pen... These were some sounds of home, but there is more.

Home was a catalog of memories in scattered sequence such as that time in April when Randy and I cranked a road grader and plowed up a good stretch of freshly paved gravel road... That summer Sunday evening when several of us boys got caught swimming in the church's baptismal pool during the evening sermon... That time when Aunt Opal drew a bucket full of water and a rattlesnake from the well behind the house...The times when I would dig with a teaspoon for China in the shaded and soft dirt under the back porch; I would usually forget about China and concentrate on the worms I unearthed in between...The wonderfully simple Christmases when we had a three-foot-pine sapling with one strand of lights and icicles, a few wrapped packages underneath and my bicycle in the trunk of Mama's car... That time when I burst a coffee cup over a suitor's head who was cussing Mama to prove my valor. I deflated his truck tires and aimed my brother's shotgun at him, but Ida, the black baby-sitter, grabbed the gun from me; nevertheless, my actions kept Mama single for several more years... That time when Otis hooked me in the head with a treble hook while attempting to cast the lure across Collie's pond and sending me into the pond. He asked me if I was dead; I started to scare him and say yes... That time when Mama finally remarried, I threw a fit and refused to go to the ceremony and sat in the car outside the preacher's house, but I did go to the steak dinner afterwards... That time when I was six and a three-hundred-pound drainage pipe rolled over my entire body and pinned my neck back so far it almost broke. Luckily, Mama who had heard my scream came and lifted the pipe off me, a feat she hasn't accomplished since... That time when Randy, the Indian, shot me, the cowboy, in the head with a target arrow, and I wiped blood over much of the front porch area of the freshly white-washed block house...

My home was all of those things in a fixed picture frame. It was that part of my life I can never return to, nor will I ever find again. That thought both humbled and scared me. It still does.

Wearing Johnny's Shirt

Sweat softened khaki
with the fifth set of buttons
passed down from father to son to son,
hand to tractor to college.

It saw FDR, public works, and was brand new.
It knows a variety of cuss words beyond my recollection.

It fought for life and another washing in stock pens,
stitches prove it.

Hanging outside a 19 year old's britches,
it heard a fumbled proposal on Saturday afternoon
in May of '46.

It was wrapped around an 8lb. 6oz. boy
on a Wednesday morning in February
when a light blue blanket was not enough.

It listened to love songs in a pine thicket
from one who had learned that the world was more than boys,
and it reads these words over the shoulder of this generation
with no real surprise.

A Circle of Buzzards Over Highway 22

I don't think about buzzards
until I see them circling
or beside the road as I pass
standing with frustrated looks.

They seem pained at my intrusion,
want to get back to their business
in the westbound lane:
cat, 'possum, deer, or dog,
and it comes home to me
what happened when Uncle Leon
went missing on a sales trip to Florida.

The sheriff found him two weeks later
face up, his hands tied around a tree.
His wallet and eyes were gone.

If there were buzzards,
I bet when the sheriff walked up
They had that same look.

A Necessary Burden

For Chappie Bowie

I've seen the liquor bottles on your desk
like scattered chessmen
and I suppose know why
you take whiskey as a mistress,
feed on nicotine
and nod off early with no appetite.
I know the legal pad curse
prying open your eyes at 4 a.m.,
switching on the lamp,
moving your fingers in fresh usual ways,
making uneven paper piles on the bed.
I've seen you in the same change of clothes
after finally giving up and drinking coffee
in a diner near your street.

Today I read your name on a stone
with a hollow couplet attached
from someone who didn't know
you'd be spoken of less each year.
I imagine you smile at all this,
lying in your just rest
saying "Fools! Fools!"

After Supper Smoke

Night like a busy neighbor
looks over the fence at Johnny Bolton
lighting up a Camel after supper.
He smokes every night outside,
his thick brown belt undone
letting the day and evening meal settle.

In winter Johnny stays evenings
on the porch scratching
his back on a column
worn smooth on one edge
planning April, May
and laying open dirt for seed,
fertilizer from town;
the exhaled smoke loitering
beneath the tin roof.

Tonight with planting over,
Johnny picks stray tobacco
from his lip and exhales hard,
watching the smoke rise
like a prayer
spiraling in the right direction.

Auction

Wild-eyed Herefords enter;
their bellies doing a heave-ho
like water balloons suddenly nudged
by a curious finger.

Packed into the ring,
pushing sidewalls and each other
trying to find a flaw and deliverance,
their fear floats up off the sawdust
as bellows and spit slung from white faced lips.

This scene and the smell of manure goes unnoticed
into seasoned men's faces either tanned or reddish
according to brimmed hats or liquor
who signal with a nod, yell, or 2 fingers to the temple
a bid.

Straight-faced, these windblown and wiregrass men sit
Like a gambler holding a flush,
putting fate in a prayer on Sunday;
the short term in the loins of a good bull.

Blues Chant

Got the blues:
the filled up with pancakes blues,
the see a man pissin' in the alley mankind blues,
the just told a lie they took it for the truth blues,
the broken shoe string and I'm late blues,
the guest in the bathroom no toilet tissue blues.

Got the blue blues:
the rat across the floor roach in the cabinet blues,
the face to face wide open zipper blues,
the unsigned invitation RSVP blues,
the dragging tailpipe 1992 Impala blues,
the only thing on this bone is fat blues.

Yes sir, the blues:
the please check the number and redial blues,
the bust my ass on the ice wore the wrong shoes blues,
the perked all night taste bitter and gives me gas coffee blues,
the lust blues must blues,
the trailing out fading out three dots and I know there's more blues blues.

C.B. Warren's Shotgun

It stands in a corner of the back room
the 12 gauge hampered by blue black soot,
old enough to need encouraging.

Bobby Lee with a butch haircut fingers
the wood around the window pane;
cricket wings aren't scrubbing,
diesels take other highways;
this quiet is too severe.

What is it?
Noiseless in the pasture,
Sitting high in the old water oak?
Dammit, show your face!

The shells in Papa's dresser,
a 12 gauge loaded is a 12 gauge proud
to Bobby Lee with a butch haircut.

It scratched the screen,
Pulled on the door;
Papa's working at the mill;
Bobby Lee is the man.

Loud orange splashes the dark;
no reflection,
no wings scrub;
Dammit, show your face!

Church Day, Conway, Arkansas

This morning, my faith rusty,
I stand in front of Conway Baptist
like a farm team outfielder
finally getting called up.
This church, strong and bricked,
oak doored and last noticed on Saturday night
when my reverence was lowering a long neck
after a long taste,
hoping God wasn't looking
or appreciated my small guilt.

This morning, not bright and blue,
with some sun and Laura urging me
toward those big doors and grace,
I stand next to her in black
and the Lord on the cross,
both strong as new rope.

Dry Times

Red road dust billows from mud-grip tires
choking fence and tree alike.
A lone cow coughs in the pasture;
manure rots straightway.
In this drought I am confused,
seek lower damper ground.
I was born in wetness to die in dust;
'54 is the devil's year.

Empty Canteen

Other than dust lying
like powder in the bedroom closet
was the scrubbed silver flask
Daddy carried on Guam
standing battle proud
as if it remembered
its hip position and contents
were a soldier's cross in full view,
or when the neat crease near the cap
meant a jap bullet ricocheted
from a scared private's blood
when war came between heaven
and that empty canteen.

Flat Stones Skip Then Stall

Poised at the edge of Collie Cleghorn's blue
black pond
a bare chested tough nut boy rears back,
lets go rocks toward the brown water log islands
where turtles gather to sun.

Then sure as a rock lands short
they disappear into the back pasture's wet eye.
Here with no movement,
no still targets on the logs,
the boy hunts flat stones
as the old pond dangles
its cool mystery before him,
tugs on his green-eyed appetite for wonder.

He throws these new slick stones
one after the other,
each time bending farther
letting them go side-armed and smooth
skip-plop-skip-plop
mainly chances to fail.

Empty handed now
figuring the number
of skims to the accidentally placed log
he gathers a fresh handful of smooth rocks
and practices.

Explaining Fall

Sashaying down in a reign of amber and gold,
autumn leaves aren't the highlight of October.

They don't compare to Harry Bowen
stiff-arming a linebacker from Valdosta
 when all that's falling is opposing coach's faces,
streamers from blue and white pom-poms,
and coke cup confetti.

Harry's heard this on Saturday mornings
after the team breakfast and game film
in the barber shop among older crew cut men
who sit shadowed behind the sign,
Blue Devil booster, Close early for out of town games.

They sit going over each play,
second guessing the coach on runs with no gain
"Hell that number 88 was wide open over the middle.

Man can that boy run, should've thrown it to him."
The same talk carries over
to church where the Reverend Dewey Jones preaches

red faced and proud on the game of life
and how the Blue Devils won at least one.

Harry takes this in little at a time,
understanding when deacons slap him on the back
 saying "damn good game, Son"
that they wish they were
 the tailback going off tackle
or sliding a hand under a letter jacket
too big for the girl it covered
who kissed good.
Harry knows this is their way
of explaining fall.

Giving Miller Williams a Ride

I picked up Miller Williams
for his reading at the college
Flannery O'Connor went to.
There was no symbolism to his room,
108 at the Comfort Inn and Suites
when I arrived scared.

Knocking on the door,
I waited in blazer and tie;
He opened it in good slacks and a corduroy coat.
Eyeing me through those thick glass lenses,
he stuck out his hand that I shook firmly
hoping he noticed.

Inside, yellow sheets of paper littered the floor.
He noticed me noticing;
simply said practice.

During the reading I watched
the shock on faces from the line,
I lie on my wife and imagine yours
wondering what other scenes were deleted
from all those lines and lives
crumpled in a yellow heap
beside that motel bed.

Learning What to Ignore

Start easy with scientific explanations,
Dr. Wilson's lectures on the three types of matter;
remember that iced tea is sweet
and wet and right in August,
that red wood is scarce and takes time,
that gas in middle school is often funny;
then move on.
Learn not to look at car wrecks,
metal and flesh gone haywire;
keep your eyes on the road
or you might recognize a neighbor
or be next.
Don't stare at those twisted at birth
with high foreheads or crooked limbs,
unless you can offer assistance,
or they'll trouble you deep.
Forget the obvious;
habit has its own hard clock.
Facts will remain;
Dr. Wilson made sure.
Move on.

I Went Home Early

I, a secret wish
often discussed in blue ribbon bars
between cut shots on felt covered slate,
was sired in darkness, in sweat, in Tulsa
by motions similar to the oil derrick
nodding in Uncle Frank's front yard;
was dropped from black Oklahoma
to gnat south Georgia,
fresh manure and fried chicken,
to grow like goat grass
to sixteen years,
to a city beside I-75
with Holiday Inn, Kiwanis, and Baptists.

There with a gator on my shirt
and oil in my loins from Oklahoma,
in the midst of God's hot breath
in a Mustang;
mature breasts thrust into my hands,
into my …
I went home early.

Home to the land of you-uns and thars,
to clap thunder and dogs whining at the door,
to mountain ash and moonshine
rougher than pine tree bark,

to where brown trout await floating bait
like deacons for the plate.

Look for the Brief Release

It's Monday,
I scratched my loafer on uneven cement,
took a deep Jack LaLane breath,
smelled the jack hammer's rough pollen,
sneezed.
The next day I saw a Buick
wrapped around a telephone pole
and hair suddenly grown,
blowing in shattered glass,
remembered the old line about sudden stops,
accelerated.
On Wednesday I use the Gulf Station john
recognized my high school sweetheart's name
on the stall,
She takes black or white;
washed my hands.
Thursday, the dentist said I needed a root canal,
asked my wife to wear the silk night gown
I bought her in St. Thomas,
performed.
Then Friday, it's the odd week with no
paycheck,
I grabbed a Bud at a bar where I used to drink
underage,
shook the damp hand that still doesn't know me,
drank another.

The weekend, Saturday, oh hell,
raked the yard, each stroke drowning
my cuss words for the quick winds of October,
broke the handle.
Sunday, the collection plate heading my way
I dropped in a note written on a check stub;
whispered, *we're square, Jesus.*

MARTA Monologue

I be,
with essence, man
I am,
damn right,
cold blooded,
for real.
I got what it takes
to be a dream,
somebody unh-hunhed
when I pass,
clean, Baby,
with bad sweatin' out
of my forehead,
100% man,
sponged.
I got ideas,
you know,
conversation;
ways to get a lady
in a corner
and put her out
with my rap,
molded to her
like me
and my soul self;
'cause I'm night

walking in broad daylight,
my face-n-my shadow
the same black mirror
hangin' in tight,
freelance,
and fine.

Mercy, Good Buddy

3:16 a.m.;
the pictures taken,
the chalk lines drawn,
post mortem activity finished,
cancelled by Fords pulling Airstream trailers
on the interstate toward Phoenix.

Certainly someone saw Virgil Simmons
pull onto the safety lane to change
his flat right front.

With a back now straightened by a truss,
his left leg stiff in a brace
growing on him, with him since DaNang in '68,
Virgil's been trained to fend for himself,
summon help when the task requires;
"Mercy, good buddy."

Two men with close cropped hair
are proud of their berets
and out to prove it,
loosen lug bolts, skin, and bone
from Virgil's forehead and torso.

Lying in ditch water
with weeds like rice stalks

feeling his life run out,
hearing trailers heading west to Phoenix;
mercy, good buddy.

Linger

Because I'm drunk
and you can't drive a straight shift,
linger.

We can sleep tonight
in the back seat,
count the stars
in the rear window
and know why constellations
draw men to the moon.
We can undress,
search each other's skin
for moles and scars,
learn about heredity
and bicycle wrecks,
or sit here naked in the night
as pale outlines
trying the usual hand on thigh
until we tire and fall asleep.

Because we are almost strangers,
linger.

Nightwalkers

Nobody moves long this night
in July without stopping,
taking out a rag
wiping their forehead,
the back of the neck
before moving on.
 Night doesn't scare them,
but heat does;
especially these men
wearing your donated clothes
walking in reclaimed shoes
toward the cool hours before day;
 the air thick and damp
as a preacher's hand,
their eyes like closets
cleaned out.

On the Old Ocilla Highway

"There's Power in the Blood"

Mornings mixed with sunshine and drizzle,
nothing new to the old Ocilla Highway.
A welcomed wetness confines flies, gnats and
livestock odors;
men with fair, leather-like faces pause,
see the sun with itchy palms;
there's power in the blood,
40 acres to plow 'fore dinner.

Once a 5 a.m. ritual of hitchin' mules
to a wood and iron turning plow
begins these days at 6:30;
keys fit ignitions of Massey Fergusons, John
Deeres,
all aluminum, iron and rubber
made nimble by power steering, power take off,
and 12-14 foot harrows;
strength inherited from leather reins
appears in black diesel smoke,
felt in vibrations knocking dew from a wet
morning seat.

"We Will Gather at the River"

Men baptized in day long sweat
draw strength from 18 forward gears
and a ton-n-a-half of peanuts to the acre.
They know almanacs, the 6 o'clock news from
Albany,
Sunday sermon signs, and fertilizer;
marry women named Effie Jo, LaRue, and Irene
who are man strong with short fingernails,
who birth stout sons and big-boned daughters.
All are obedient;
all are Baptist.

They have put in a day
when angus bulls bellow in heat
and pine trees stand shadowed.
Lights die early after appetites;
Days begun with man-made power
rest with the Lord
on the old Ocilla Highway.

Or Its Equivalent

See him,
age 48,
an explosion
of arms, legs,
his whole body
wrestling short tantrums,
tied down with wide belts,
shot up with a needle
full of calm down.

He bows and exhales
as if pins puncture each organ
or some hunter
is jumping a covey
of quail in his lungs.

He tears at himself
Like a dog with red mange,
clawing for death
or its equivalent
mercy.

Out on a Limb

A fat squirrel inches out
toward the slim end of the limb
and due to gravity and grip is lowered
onto another equally limber level.
So goes the process down
to the bottom where he scurries back
to the hole in the trunk
where a branch was before
sudden August lightning took it.

This is the fat boy's well stocked shelter.
Of course, all descending is according to law;
this gravity requires a proportion I outgrew
and at eight had underestimated
when I crawled out on an oak limb
thinking my chances better until
a quick crack dropped me 12 feet to packed dirt
and all the air burst out of me
in a loud HUMPH!

The air came back to see if the squirrel was
gone
as I watched fat boy carry more acorns home

Position Matters

With a loaf of bread, bologna, and 2 Budweisers
the lint haired negro at the Kroger
waiting for the register to open knows.

With teased hair and her boyfriend
tore up with lust beside her,
the woman behind the steering wheel knows,
and the mannequins in the Macy's window
somehow know that everywhere:
subway, fast food toilet, Dodge truck bed on
Friday night,
position matters;
determines escape.

In church Johnny Bolton sits next to the aisle,
drives with his left hand mostly on the door
handle,
leaves the backdoor cracked in February.
On the radio he's heard what others fear:
UFO's in Kansas, heartless cow carcasses in
Colorado,
daily doses of bizarre.

On a sidewalk bench near the Catholic Church
a man eats fried chicken from a box,
going over his plan and each bone slow,
his eyes teasing passersby

and right then
I know.

Prayer

With head in hand, Lord, allow me
to sift my sins and make smooth
the knots of my past like flour
shaken and slung into a pan for kneading.

Let me prop my feet on the cold
floor mornings of adolescence
when heat was a dream I woke to
and went through the day with
from radiator to Rachel.

Forgive, Father, my nature to question
the ticklish definitions of faith
when winding west on State 76
a Methodist daughter made suggestions
not understood then…Just As I Am, all jokes
aside.

Hear this not just for me
but for others similarly inclined.
Understand, please, those suffering powerless
blood,
Not death ready but narrow as light poles
Sunk deep in hope and a week's check.

Lord, grant me relief;
a place in the shade on fresh straw,
a dirt road showered in honeysuckle
so I can meet you head on.

Yes, dear Jesus, I pray;
grant me gospel.

Private Pilot

For Brad Pope

He looks away
from the controls of the Cessna
down at the flat green trees,
black plowed dirt, hayfield browns,
and blues for water.
The horizon, altimeter, and fuel
consumption not his concern.

Water towers mean towns,
maybe women in dresses,
men in laced shoes, and children;
most won't look up or know they're smaller
than they think they are.

Pure Attraction

There's a pull to old ponds;
that draw you right out of dungarees in May,
right out of flour sack print shirts
and fruit of the looms into their caramel eye.
Red-eye perch kiss your shin at the warm edge,
usher you into the cool pupil for one purpose

Sister Rachel

Think how lines, the broken and express lines
meandering across the palm
mean something about old nights, new ones,
car wrecks and bank accounts;
how a pumice stone or acid could alter
existence.
Think about signs in small towns, in
newspapers,
Know Your Future! Registered Palmist!
Throw out visions of bandanaed heads, broken
teeth,
or walking though beads into a back room;
risk the truth.

West of Gray, Georgia, Sister Rachel lives
in a brick house with no porch,
though Rachel, big-boned red headed Rachel,
wearing initialed glasses is gracious,
accepts two twenties,
accepts the mission of mystery.

No inner sanctum with dull lights
or card table covered in madras,
but more like an office
beyond a ping-pong table to a business desk,
put both arms palms up on waxed hardwood.

Here she draws a bespeckled bead on your future;
notice the odor,
a clue sweating out of the mortar,
and feel your blood warm,
heating up an answer.

Now demand Rachel put the blue light on
what will happen.
Pull it over. Frisk it;
take it downtown, lock it up,
but give you the handcuff key.
 Bear down as she releases
the secrets of ripples and creases;
wonder if there's some script with laws and givens
spelling out longevity, cash flow, child gender;
wonder if Sister Rachel cares like the sign
near her house says Jesus does;
wonder when customers meet a short end
where to place blame.

Suppose It's True After All What Then

So say the orange pamphlets raining down
on rock music lovers gathered at Byron,
and the white shirt and blue pants Mormans
pumping schwinns and God all over town,
and the just released juvenile offender
starting out loud in Central City Park
with a pulpit voice and stiff bible.

Whiskered country singers after love,
cheating and beer close their shows
with a hymn to show good faith and plant hope.
Missionaries learn to hoe and irrigate,
speak Spanish or a tribal tongue,
instill with deeds and antibiotics a message,
a new-fangled hocus-pocus
without feathers, chants, and rattles.

Suppose it's True

That fish were first,
that vowels and consonants stuck men
with a language for coming to terms
with failure,
with mystery;
that what's under pepsi bottle caps
says something fresh about spirit.

After All

the five and ten-dollar bills gently put
in the church plate by people
serious about heaven;
or when an x-box sticks out
more than scripture.

What Then
Grace?
Or just the ability to laugh
at your broken shoe lace.

Straight Plow

Furrowed, red oak handle,
useless these many years,
stands out of the way
beside bridle, bit, and blinder
without mule, cuss words, thin leather strap
or Johnny's broad hands to guide it, turn it,
plant it deep in brown loam
at the start of each row's journey.

That

Don't turn around.
I know your face:
the O'Hara mole,
the right chin,
the eyes,
green-gray,
the lids relaxed.
But your neck
(don't turn)
The nape
terraced;
the hair
escaping the bun;
that,
lady,
woman,
lover,
that.

The Last Time Mama Looked at Her Son

Was in February;
the snow, a comfort to some, deep and
annoying;
two full weeks without a thaw;
the wind making swirling sounds
like cars meeting at high speeds.

He stood at the door to her room,
her bed stuck between cardboard boxes
of memorabilia and old skirts, blouses and print
dresses.
Touching her arm below the elbow she stirred
and knew him,
her eyes adjusting to the night light.
Seeing pain at work in her eyes.
he remembered her brief romance
with the grocery store butcher;
she was a cashier, convenient,
smiling at customers regardless.
He thought of the time at the bus station;
Her drawing on a Lucky Strike,
wondering if her "ex" had soaked my mind
with someday Son this will all be yours.
He understood her squeezing his fingers
that same night he cried for daddy.

He left her mumbling 'night, Son,
found his bed and began wrestling
new, lean memories.

The Likeness at the End of the Line

Under the state road bridge,
car and tractor-trailer tires slapping
the seams in the concrete above,
he sits in overalls and half laced boots,
smelling like the dough balls and chicken hearts
in separate stacks beside him.

A weathered cane pole and cheap rod-n-reel prop
on fresh cut y-shaped oak limbs,
nylon lines disguised by and disappearing
into lightly rippled water.

Today it's neither crappie schooling
just below the surface
nor the bigmouth feeding on silver minnows
outside the shade of the bridge,
but the flathead cotton-bellied mystery
waiting on a strong scent
in the cold black bottom water.

Fishing deep then he places hope
in the odor of bait
spit on for luck,
stuck tight around the certainty
of pointed steel to lure him,

hook him,
hold him
on his reluctant trip
to a face whiskered
like his own.

The Baby in the Other Room

The baby lies on goose down
flailing silently at the night,
asking those beginning questions:
Why is night black?
Where are mother's breasts?
What is alone?

Tiny fat feet kick,
keeping the monsters at bay,
parrying the dark
incessantly 'til dawn:
Why is night black?

The Master's Touch

Whisper selfish prayers
for Mama at her bedside,
lying as a posture pale, swollen
draped in hospital cotton.
"Lord, drain this poison from her soul."
Preachers failed,
and the layman's function cracked
by sudden August lightning.
A forefinger can't support a limber dyke;
Providence is such a slippery eel

The Point of Spring

is in the speech of flowers
piped through bees and it's happy
even when the bee bogs down
into a base drone,
gets stuck in a chrysanthemum's propaganda,
secrets are being passed on,
forwarded to us in code,
and we must listen.
What we're hearing are the flower's clues
for the bees extrication;
they could make a difference in our own.

The Senses Sometime Explode

Seeing some dislocated funk
overalled and t-shirted swigging
cheap stuff in the night light alley
behind the good stores downtown.

Hearing thank you Jesus,
thank you Jesus from caved-in souls
sashaying their uplifted bones and tambourines
in a canvas tent beneath heaven.

Smelling a stockyard's boiled hog hair
slipping from pork pores;
tasting tomatoes just picked tartness
twisting lips as a way of saying surprise.

Touching you, sleeping, near the temples
where fine shaded hair begins,
and that for those few moments
is enough.

The Water That Persuades

On the last Sunday in May in Turner County,
cars and trucks full of the week weary
cover paved and red dirt roads;
all sinners coming to witness the power of water,
of white starch turned liquid
on the backs of those old enough to know
the blood shame puddled
in a cool place behind Johnny Bolton's barn.

The morning before thick dew settled
on cow backs, stacked peanut hay bales
left in the field;
three boys got nasty with a bone handled knife,
held a pig spread eagle
and got carried away,
making a boar a shoat;
the blood of lost litters running down
onto six excited hands;
the shoat screaming at an even higher pitch.

Today Elmer Bullington raises his limber King James,
asking if there are any among you;
there are: Ronnie, Randy, and me;
the pigs fear vibrating through our knees,

tapping out a prayer that we be forgiven,
turnt loose from last night's dreams of high shrills.

We stand bare chested in black pants and bare feet
in the pool above the choir humming "Just As I Am;"
the preacher announcing this occasion in the name
of Father, Son, and Holy Ghost,
men I'm certain we hardly knew.
Randy says, "it's cold,"
as he's dipped and rinsed of sin.
"This water's cold!"

This Last Fine Fact

This morning as you finger the neat white buttons
before someone with pale hands buttons them for you,
think of those things that are automatic
like brushing your teeth
or putting your Buick in drive;
then press on:
back through the first October leaf falling,
through the kiss you knew was real
and settled things,
or the first time you sat heavy in church;
Just As I Am you thought,
does God buy wholesale?

Now go back to beginnings,
to science,
the bastard child of Genesis,
the dammed up river of the mind,
and everything starts to shake:
hair dryers and faucet water become larger,
explained, believed,
displaced from the magnetism of mystery.
You stand, walk, and work in a world

whose fulcrum is an off/on switch.

Only at night does mystery return,
standing, say, on a flat road east of Jackson
trying to flag some salesman down.
You're coming to a place where you can't tell.
History is a rug pulled out from under you.
You recall overlooked facts:
Martin Luther's problem with money,
Patton's ability to recite poetry.
Realize what we come to,
we come to.
Most want to go back, regroup, reclaim.
Some don't.
Watch them;
they're our hope.

The Wind Across Arkansas

I hear you
coming west from Memphis,
coming like the train from D.C.,
coming to separate fish flopping on the bank
of a farm pond near Helena
near dark.

Coming, yes-sir, coming
to hover over industry in Texarkana,
coming to steal the sewer and stockyard stench,
carry it like a crop duster to noses in Springdale
that are used to it or frown and go indoors.

Coming, by God, Coming
to plow through Dumas
like a team of spooked mules
scaring us into shelters;
a few into graves.

Then coming,
coming back
to move among the faces of Little Rock
as steam from a busy lunch kitchen,
learning as many secrets as possible.

We Still Chew Cannonball

Teeth stained a cure tobacco color;
men in khakis with rolled up sleeves
showing forearms with bleached hairs
grizzled as those on an old sow's back;
fear nothing but God and late frosts.
      Deacon men, diesel men
rest easy in winter,
quote beef prices after Wednesday's sale,
build on to barns not low and red,
but creosote and tin
let the worked dirt breath this fallow season
before struggling with watermelon vines,
choking on peanut picker dust.
      Pray day, wash away
the dew baptizes thee;
tractors left dormant awake once more
waiting on orders like well trained hounds.
An annual glint burns hard in Hamp Smith's eyes
in a kitchen outside Ocilla
is of the soil,
is of the soul;
he's up early
chewing Cannonball.

Whoa Night

A slack season complete with November moods
when the soul carries a sulphur stench
as if a match were struck;
yet there's the modest humidifier
promised in the last week of December:
sippin' whisky before a slow burning, fresh cut hickory log,
delusions of grandeur at the Wexler's on the 31st,
destroying enough braincells to lust for the wife of 20 years;
Relief,
Finally relief;
Jim Beam where have you been?

A road dark as greasy fingernails;
Leaves like curtains are gone.
The moon like a dogwood bloom
orphaned in the night.
Doves shot at sundown
In a baited millet field.
What a welcome!

How do you decide it's finished?
When dreams become the color of coffee stains?
Or is it easy

like a virgin saying, "what the hell, I'm 18, my
vote counts!"
What are the terms?
Will the soul be bartered this night
like baseball cards in the 4th grade?
A Mickey Mantle for a Willie Mays,
both respected hitters;
seems fair.
A head for a heart, quill for a pen?
Not likely.

Whoa night,
don't fail me now, Jim Beam.

When We Can't Find the Handle

On clear Saturday nights
when the regulars gang up
at Johnny's Juke Joint and Bar to laugh
at each other's failures
one will get bent,
get fed up with life, wife, or job,
let the curr dog loose
that's baring its teeth in his blood
and throw a roundhouse right that connects.

We all come apart;
eventually catch our finger in the door and lash
out,
explode like a drained beer bottle
dropped on the highway,
sling anything and cuss words and tears
we get our bruised hands on.
Tonight there're witnesses
standing out front who understand
this is a form of redemption.

www.ingramcontent.com/pod-product-compliance
Lightning Source LLC
Chambersburg PA
CBHW051714040426
42446CB00008B/873